MW01075785

The Bar Exam is Easy

by Kris Rivenburgh

The Bar Exam is Easy

Copyright © 2012 Kris Rivenburgh

Coffee Publishing

Edited by Susan I. Ullrich

All rights reserved. No part of this publication may be reproduced or distributed in any form or by any means, or stored in a database or retrieval system, without the prior written permission of the author.

ISBN: 9781980621645

Brandon M. Smith @BMSmith829 · 29 Oct 2014
@krisrivenburgh Your bar exam book was gold. After so much frustration/wasted effort, your streamlined approach is what I needed. THANK YOU!

       1   ...

Nick Shook @Shicholas · 13m
@krisrivenburgh your advice in the "Bar Exam is Easy" was money. Thank you so much!

Expand   Reply Retweet Favorite More

 Angie @headliner2 · 43m

Thanks to @thebariseasy I passed the tx bar exam on the first try! Anyone who is taking the bar this is a must read book!

    1   ★ 1   ...

 Char_C @charchinn · 5h
@thebariseasy great book!!! #july2015

 1   ★   ...

DEDICATION

To Archer, my cinnamon dog.

CONTENTS

DISCLAIMER

In a cruel twist of fate, you (and you alone) are responsible for your own performance on the bar exam.

This book is opinion based on the author's experience with the Texas Bar Exam.

Surprisingly, the author has not spent his life studying the testing areas and exam details for all 50 states.

It is highly recommended that you consult multiple resources on how to best study for your state's bar exam.

THINK DYNAMICALLY

Everyone that gave me advice on taking the bar exam told me to take a bar review course.

The general message:

Don't try to be a hero. Don't outsmart yourself. Don't cheap out now (after paying 6-figures in tuition). Just go buy a course and do what they say.

This advice came from esteemed attorneys and professors.

And I listened. And I was wrong to do so.

We have a way of getting brainwashed and not seeing things for what they really are.

My well-intentioned advisors were just echoing what had worked for them and so many others: You take a course, you do what they say, and you pass.

Still, my eyes were narrowed at the bar prep courses. Seemingly everyone endorsed them but I wasn't sold on their effectiveness.

How come the pass rates were so mediocre if these bar courses were so golden?

Also, there were a lot of grubby commercial vibes coming from those bar course tables. Kind of like MLM

Tupperware party energy but more academic and official.

Despite my suspicions, I fell for the ruse. #socialproof

A lot of my cash was sacrificed to the bar prep deities.

And a lot of my time and energy was lost into the ether for no good reason.

I wrote this book to tell you, to urge you that there is a better way; I hope to unwind a lot of the brainwashing you've been inundated with since you first heard about the bar exam.

Right now, you might be where I was, lost in the micro of the moment. If you can, extract yourself and see if you can't form a semblance of the macro.

The micro is a small slice of time where uncertainty reigns supreme and our psychological makeup makes us susceptible to influence (because it's just a small moment in time).

The macro is where take a step back and look at the big picture so we can ascertain what's really happening and make sound decisions (because we're able to put things in their context over the long run).

It's critical that you're able to think dynamically and not linearly because we are in a dynamic environment.

Linear thinking makes you a follower of instruction.

Dynamic thinking allows you to figure out your environment and achieve a high degree of alignment with those things that are in it so you can act accordingly.

For the purposes of this book this means understanding how to best approach the bar exam for YOU.

Maybe a bar course is indeed the right path for how you're wired and you decide to take one.

That's 100% fine.

But what I don't want is for you to fall for the bar prep myth just because you've been scared to death by chants of "the bar exam is hard" for the last 5 years.

AUTHOR'S NOTE

The first error-laden digital copy of The Bar Exam is Easy made its way onto Amazon in mid-2012.

The good thing about e-books is you always have the luxury of editing and re-publishing with only the previous buyers worse for wear.

As such, I've continually updated this book to account for feedback I've received and the addition of Federal Civil Procedure to the exam.

But after this copy hits the press and goes into bookstores across the world, everything will be set in stone.

So once the bar examiners come out with their next arbitrary change to make it look like they're actually doing something (the bar exam has no nexus to practicing law), just remember the recommendations and overriding theme set forth in this book and adjust accordingly.

If a significant change comes to my attention, I'll provide thoughts on TheBarIsEasy.com.

"You have nothing to fear except for things that are scary."

WHY YOU SHOULD READ THIS BOOK

- Save Time
- Save Money
- Gain Confidence
- Make Your Life Easy
- Pass the Bar Exam

In this book, I walk right up to the bar exam store, pick up a cinder block, and throw it as hard as I can into the window. I don't shatter the glass for the sake of being a contrarian. I shatter the glass because it needs to be shattered.

You should read this book - at the very least - to gain the perspective you will not hear. You've heard how hard the bar exam is from everyone else. Why not hear how easy the bar exam is from someone who took and passed the February 2012 Texas Bar Exam?

FYI: I graduated from a tier four law school and finished in the bottom 50% of my class. Neither mattered.

INTRODUCTION

The bar exam is easy.

I failed the Texas Bar Exam twice before I passed on the third try.

The first time I took the exam I scored a 637. The second time I took the bar exam I scored a 654. The third time I took the bar exam I scored a 706. Passing is a 675.

So if the bar exam is so easy, why did I fail twice?

The answer boils down to this:

The first two times I wasted too much time and mental energy going through bar prep fluff.

The third time I developed and executed a simple study plan.

In two minutes, I will share this plan with you. If you

follow my plan, you will likely pass and you will not need to spend thousands of dollars for a bar review course. Not only will you save money, but you will save dozens of hours in precious, precious time.

I will discuss in detail:

- How to virtually guarantee you will pass the bar
- How much time you should study for each day
- What study materials you need
- When you should start studying
- What to do during test days
- Practical prep tips that will make your life easy
- What your MBE practice scores should look like
- How many MBE questions you should do
- What your mindset should be
- What the bar exam is like

Even if you're not taking the Texas Bar Exam, the basic strategy and principals in this book will apply to most, if not all, bar exams.

The Myth, The Legend

The bar exam is big business and bar review courses love for bar exam myths to be perpetrated.

They love for professors to freak their students out.

They love for law students and lawyers to carry the myth on.

They love for family members and friends to repeat the legends.

"The bar exam is the hardest test ever."

The way everyone talked up the exam, I thought I was headed into a room where a 76-year-old hardened legal warden flipped open a thick, dusty book and asked me to recite 50 oral essays.

Instead, the bar exam was a simple, straightforward test. And for whatever it's worth, the Texas Bar Exam has one of the lower passage rates.

I failed the bar exam twice because I didn't study the stupid way for enough hours. It took me two times around but I finally realized bar review courses are wholly inefficient (they waste time and money).

The best thing out of the bar review courses is the study materials – and I only needed four books (most only need three) out of everything they gave me to pass the third time.

You might think the cumulative knowledge of preparing twice played a large role in passing the third time. This was not the case. Here's why:

First, there were significant gaps of time between when I took the exam. The dates of my bar examinations were July 2010, July 2011, and February 2012.

Second, my MBE practice scores started off at the same clip during my third attempt as they had the previous two. Similarly, my practice essays were only marginally better off on my third attempt.

Third, my last bar exam score jumped 69 points from my first exam and 52 points from my second exam. This extreme point differential is too large to be explained away by previous bar experience.

CH 1: GENERAL ADVICE

Before you read my specific techniques and recommendations for studying, I want you to stop and realize that the bar exam is pass/fail. This means you either get a P or an F. This means striving for perfection is a waste of time!

Throughout our education, we've been assigned a specific letter or number grade after a test, so we're trained to try to get an A. It's not the same on the bar exam. On the bar exam, a passing score passes you whether it's on the exact cutoff or 100 points above.

So when you're studying or even taking the test, don't worry about the little stuff. You're just trying to do well on most of the material; it's a holistic thing.

This means don't waste your time on learning every last exception to the law. This means don't spend five minutes answering one MBE question. This means don't give equal study time to essay subjects that have only been tested once.

Focus on what's typically on the exam. Focus on the marquee test areas.

Key Jurisdictional Notes

It is vital that you understand how your state tests and scores the bar exam. This information will be on the official state bar exam website. Pay particular attention to:

- How MBE, MPT, essays, and any other sections are weighted
- Whether you need a minimum score on essays or MBE to pass
- Whether points scored on the MBE or essays can compensate for one another (i.e., can you make up ground on the MBE with essays?)
- Whether essays are state-specific or multistate

Always factor your jurisdiction's policies into consideration when determining your study plan.

The Bar is Easy Effect

You should be aware that just as bar takers read this book, so do bar examiners. Bar examiners may not like the fact that I'm pointing one of those big, yellow foam hands at the bar exam and saying, "Here's how you do it the easy way."

Just as a warning: Things may change in some jurisdictions because of this book. For example, different or rarely tested subjects may show up on your exam.

However, by and large, the bar exam is going to remain

the same. You will have a very difficult time failing if you follow my advice, but I'd like to recommend you also keep rarely tested subject areas on your radar just in case.

As an example of change, look at what happened on the July 2012 Michigan Bar Exam. The statewide passage rate tanked to 55%. The lowest cumulative pass rate in the previous 6 years was 72%. Clearly, the bar examiners switched things up.

I by no means am suggesting my book had anything to do with the change. What I am saying is bar examiners can and do change the exam.

Don't freak out on this update. The bar exam is still a pass/fail minimal competency test with the same major testing areas popping up over and over. They can only modify the subject matter so much.

To safeguard against what happened in Michigan, critically read over your state's official bar exam website. Don't gloss over an update notice, even if it's a casual one. Additionally, I would contact the bar examiners and specifically ask whether any substantive changes or updates have been made to the bar exam.

The best and most important source of information is always your state's official bar exam website. Read it.

If anything is ever unclear, don't hesitate to ask for a clarification.

CH 2: THE MULTISTATE

The multistate bar exam (MBE) is 200 multiple choice questions. The MBE on the bar exam is divided up into two three-hour sessions. Each session will have 100 questions. With the MBE, you can rack up a lot of baseline points and give yourself cushion on the essays.

The MBE style and format are the same for everyone in the nation. I'm not sure if everyone gets the same MBE questions, but the types of questions are all the same.

With MBE questions, you're either right or you're wrong. You can't get any partial points like you can on the essays.

When you study for the MBE, don't you dare ever waste one second watching a video over the MBE. Watching videos to prepare for the MBE is a poor use of time.

To study for the MBE, the only thing you need to do is practice MBE questions. The more questions you practice, the more likely you are to pass.

(I get emails on this all the time and, yes, that's really all you need to do.)

What I mean by practicing questions is that you read the question, answer it, and then read the answer explanation and understand why you got it right or wrong.

To make sure you dominate the MBE, practice 2,200 questions spread across all the subjects. Practicing 2,200 questions may sound like a mountain but it's only an average of 55 questions per day over the course of 40 days (just an illustration, not a recommendation).

The subjects are: Contracts, Torts, Property, Criminal Law and Procedure, Constitutional Law, Evidence, Federal Civil Procedure.

Note: I count Criminal Law and Criminal Procedure as one subject because they are treated as one subject on the MBE in terms of representation. Stated another way, Criminal Law and Criminal Procedure combined have the same number of questions as Torts or any other subject.

Bar courses waste your time in teaching you these subjects. They will give you a 3-4-hour lecture video on each subject along with an outline for you to go over. You may also be presented with a 3-4-hour video reviewing every question and answer on a practice test.

The last thing you need to do is waste your valuable study time reviewing these entire subjects and/or spend four minutes reviewing every question.

The only time watching a video snippet would make sense is if you still don't understand why a correct answer is correct after reading the explanation.

The intelligent way to study is to dive right into the sample MBE questions. By going through the questions, you learn both the pertinent law and how it will be tested on the exam.

Contrast practicing what's actually on the exam against attempting to master an entire subject. The practice will not only be more efficient, but more effective. In the end, you score more points while saving time and conserving brain power.

How to Study

When you first start studying, go through eight questions from one subject as if you were taking the exam. Then, compare the correct answer and explanation to ensure you understand the question and answer completely. Once you finish this process for all eight questions, move on to the next subject.

Understanding the reasoning behind the right answer is important. It's not enough that you get the right answer. You must also know *why* you got the right answer. If you got it wrong, you obviously need to compare the reasoning, but you might find that you actually had the reasoning correct and just read the question too fast.

Tip: The best way to figure out how the bar examiners try to fool you on the MBE is by getting burned first hand. Reading about their tricks helps but experiencing them is the best education. After all, we don't really know the stove is hot until we touch it (or at least get close enough to feel the heat).

The reason you check the answers and explanations after each subject is because the fact patterns are still fresh in your mind. If you go through all the questions from all the subjects and then check all the answers afterwards, you forget fact patterns, why you picked certain answers, etc. Then you have to reread questions and familiarize yourself with them which wastes time.

It's really important to track your percentages (per subject and overall) as you go so you have a good gauge of where you're at, how much you're progressing, and whether you need to allot extra time to particular subjects. Keeping stats also adds an element of fun and intrigue to MBE practice sessions.

I recommend you start studying 10 weeks prior to the bar exam to give yourself plenty of cushion. As far as MBE questions, start your practice sessions fairly light and then slowly progress to more questions as the bar exam draws closer. Here is a sample MBE study plan:

Sample MBE Question Study Breakdown

- Weeks 1-2: 36 Questions 5x/Week For 2 Weeks = 360 questions
- Weeks 3-5: 48 Questions 5x/Week For 3 Weeks = 720 questions
- Week 6: 100 Question Simulated Exam Session (SES) on Monday, 200 Question SES on Thursday = 300 Questions
- Weeks 7-8: 60 Questions 5x/Week For 2 Weeks = 600 questions
- Week 9: 100 Question SES on Monday, Wednesday, Friday = 300 Questions

- Week 10: 48 Questions 5x/Week For 1 Week = 240 Questions

If you begin practice on the MBE 10 weeks before the bar exam and progress with the above numbers, you will complete 2,520 questions. This gives you the flexibility to take a few days off or cut short some sessions if you need a break.

In case you're wondering, practicing 2,200 questions (with 4.5 minutes to read, answer, and review) calculates out to approximately 165 hours. Prorated over 10 weeks, this comes out to roughly 2.2 hours of MBE per day.

Note: 2,200 questions is an arbitrary number. If you *only* practice 1,583 questions, by no means will you be unprepared. I urge you to strive for a higher number to throw the odds of passing wildly in your favor. The more MBE questions you practice, the more likely you will pass.

For those of you that yearn for security, practicing 2,000+ MBE questions is akin to eliminating most of your risk (of a low score) on the most important section of the bar exam.

Tip: Consistency is the key. Try to get in an MBE session at least 4 times per week (outside of the SES weeks). Even if you only muster 20 questions in a session, it's okay as long as you habitually practice MBE.

In the beginning of my MBE practice, I was averaging around 50% correct overall. By the end, I was at or above 60% overall on almost every practice session. If you get into the 65% or above range, you're doing really well.

Some subjects will give you more trouble than others. Constitutional Law and Property were my poorest subjects. I flourished in Torts.

After you finish 100 questions in each subject, you'll have a great idea of where your strengths and weaknesses are. If you're below 54% on a subject, add in five extra questions after completing your normal MBE practice routine (e.g., after completing 48 total questions, add in five more from your weak subject).

Do not sacrifice questions from your strong areas to replace them with questions from your weak areas. You want to maintain or even build upon your strengths while bringing your weak areas to average or above average.

I promise you, the more questions you practice, the better your scores will become. If your MBE scores are low or you feel unconfident, the best cure is to keep hammering away at the questions.

Answering MBE questions is the only studying you need to do for the MBE.

Think about it: The best way to study for a test is to study the material that will be on the test, NOT the subjects the test covers.

On the MBE the same concepts and fact patterns come up repeatedly. In fact, if you go through enough practice questions, you will probably see some very, very similar fact patterns and questions on the exam.

Although you may instantly recognize a fact pattern and/or question on the exam, read the question all the way through as the bar examiners may have made a small tweak that completely changes the answer.

There are only so many different ways they can test legal concepts in multiple choice questions, so if you go through 350-450 questions on each subject, you're going to have seen just about every concept and every way they can test that concept there is.

The Right Questions

It is extremely important to practice exam-level difficulty questions. Some bar prep courses start you off with easy MBE questions. For example, the question will give you a simple fact pattern and ask you to identify the legal concept illustrated. These types of questions are only marginally helpful to you. Most MBE questions on the bar exam are not this simple.

The actual bar exam questions are either multi-layered or designed to trick you. Some will seemingly have two right answers (one will be the better answer). Some will seem like a dead giveaway only to have a slight nuance in the fact pattern that gives a major misdirection. Some will require you to think through multiple legal concepts to arrive at the correct answer.

So where do you get these hard MBE questions?

You can buy good MBE practice books on Amazon and Ebay and sometimes Half Price Books and Craigslist. Before you buy, look for an indicator that the questions are similar to the ones on the bar exam. Check reviews, product descriptions, and online discussion.

MBEPracticeQuestions.com is a site that exists solely to find the best MBE workbooks on Amazon. All of my recommendations are on this site.

One more note on difficulty. MBE questions are mixed randomly throughout the test. They do not get progressively more difficult. For instance, question 200 may be a cupcake question while 167 is extremely difficult. With this in mind, don't drain excessive time on longer or more difficult questions while leaving yourself inadequate time to fully read and understand easy questions at the end of the exam.

Remember that there is no penalty for wrong answers on the MBE so don't leave any blank.

MBE Mathematical Mindset

You're not going to know the answers to all of the MBE questions. In fact, it would be amazing if you knew half of the answers. This isn't something to worry about - it's just a given.

One stats-based way of looking at the MBE is by way of percentages and points. Think about it this way: If you know 50 questions of the 200, that's 50 points you can bank. If you can narrow down 80 questions to two answers, you'll get 1/2 right which gives you another 40 points.

For the remaining 70 questions, if you can narrow 30

down to 3 questions, you'll get 10 right. And if you completely guess on the last 40, you'll tack on another 10 points.

Totaled up, that's a 110 raw score (ideally you'd like to break into the 120+ range).

Under this type of outlook, if you can just improve the number of answers you can assuredly eliminate on the MBE, your score will jump just based on the math alone. For example, if by practicing more MBE questions, you turn 20 wild guesses into 20 "50/50" answers, you just improved your score 5 points (20 complete guesses = .25 x 20 = **5 points** vs. 20 50/50s = .5 x 20 = **10 points**).

Summary

Yes, the MBE questions are tricky, but if you harden yourself to them, the test will be a breeze and you will score high. If you trudge through 2,200 bar style MBE questions on a consistent basis, the bar examiners can't throw anything at you that will faze you.

Don't study the subjects. Study the questions. The sample questions are gold. The subject outlines are fool's good.

The MBE portion of the bar exam is your foundation to a good score and the single easiest way to ensure you pass. Steadily practicing 2,200+ questions in the 2.5 months leading up to the bar exam is a recipe for success. If you want to take some insurance out on the bar exam, tack on another 400 questions.

CH 3: ESSAYS

Essays vary from state to state. Texas has 12 30-minute essays specifically over Texas law. Many other states have 6 or 8 questions either specific to the state or from the Multistate Essay Exam (MEE - consult your state's official bar exam website for what you need to study).

As I go over my experience, you will see why I believe my blueprint can save you hours of study time and actually score you more points in the end, no matter what state you're in.

After finishing day 3 of my last bar exam, I left the essay portion of the exam feeling confident that I had racked up a nice amount of points on most if not all of the 12 essays.

Was it because I mastered Texas Family Law, Business Associations, Agency, Oil and Gas, Wills and Estates, Taxation, Trusts and Guardianships, UCC, Consumer Rights, Real Property, and Bankruptcy?

No.

Was it because I took all the bar courses during law school?

No.

The reason I did well was because I studied the past 6 years' worth of essay exams and focused my attention on the subjects and concepts that were tested the most.

The first two times I studied, I watched 6-hour lectures, listened to audiobooks, and went over outlines to learn the material.

What an absolute waste of time!

Sure, I practiced essays too, but I spent more than 50% of my essay study time trying to learn the subjects. Had I concentrated 100% of my efforts into reading the past essay questions and model answers, I probably would have passed.

Don't spend 12-20 hours trying to master each essay subject. Instead, spend as many hours as you need poring over the last 10-12 years of exams.

I recommend studying exams for an average of 2 hours a day, 5 days a week, in the 2.5 months leading up to the exam. Also, work in a few simulated exam sessions (SES) amidst your regular routine to prepare yourself for exam conditions.

Sample Essay Study Breakdown

- Weeks 1-3: 2 Hour Study Sessions 5x/Week For 3 Weeks = 30 Hours
- Weeks 4: 3 Hour SES on Monday, 6 Hour SES on Thursday, 3 Hour SES on Saturday = 12 Hours
- Weeks 5-6: 2 Hour Study Sessions 5x/Week For 2 Weeks = 20 Hours
- Week 7: 3 Hour SES on Monday, 3 Hour SES on Thursday, 3 Hour SES on Saturday = 9 Hours
- Weeks 8-9: 2 Hour Study Sessions 5x/Week For 2 Weeks = 20 Hours
- Week 10: 2 Hour Study Sessions 4x/Week, 1.5 Hour Study Session 1x/Week For 1 Week = 9.5 Hours

This study plan provides for 100.5 hours of essay study. Although this may sound like a heavy workload, prorated over 10 weeks, this only amounts to roughly 1.5 hours per day.

To start studying, flip your model essay book open to the latest bar exam and work backwards from there.

You must get an essay book that has both the exam questions and the model answers. This is essential.

I studied the old exams much the same way I did the MBE questions. I read over the essay question carefully and then attempted to answer the question aloud and/or write down an answer. As exam time crept closer, I was only reading the question and then flipping to the answer, sometimes highlighting or noting important information.

During this process, you need to make sure you're not just going through the motions. By going through the motions, I mean looking at the question and answer and then saying, "yeah, I know that." The best way to check yourself is to practice two essays and then go back to the first essay and see if you can competently answer it.

(The reason you go through two essays before going back to check the answer to the first is to make sure you're retaining the information.)

On this note, I want to add that you should hammer home the law by practicing the questions multiple times – especially the questions with concepts and law that you don't grasp right away. I went through several essay questions 4 or 5 times just to make sure I knew the law and application without a hitch.

I programmed myself to know the most frequently tested areas of law that would come up. By doing this I learned the law the bar examiners wanted me to know, not the law I didn't need to know.

Writing Out Essays

I think you should write out your essay answers up to a point. Once you know how to put your answer into the proper essay format, you shouldn't continue to formally write out every last essay answer because you have a lot of essays to get through and writing them all out isn't necessary.

To reiterate, the key component here is making sure you really know the key elements/analysis. If you do and can write them out in the proper essay format, there's no need to write out 100+ essays just for writing sake.

Essays require efficiency because there are several dozen you need to get through, but you have to balance efficient practice with knowledge absorption; you should be retaining the key elements, exceptions, and analysis as you go along.

In the first 4-6 weeks of your study, I recommend writing out at least a basic answer – even if it's not formatted – just to keep yourself honest and prevent the "I knew that" delusion. But as the exam draws closer, you need to quicken your pace, at which point I recommend you transition to answering more in your head to save time and get through more essays. Just make sure you're still absorbing the material.

Tip: To better absorb the law, I pretended like the essay fact patterns involved me or people I knew in the situation. For example, I was trying to file for bankruptcy or I was the one looking for ways to legally get out of the contract, etc. It helped make the essay real for me rather than an abstract fact pattern.

Sidebar: The bar exam is about passing the test and nothing else. If you're thinking "but you don't know all the laws", spare me your semantics. Nobody knows all the laws. If for some reason you ever forget or need to brush up, it's open book for the rest of your life.

At this point, stop thinking about yourself for a second and think about the people that make and grade this thing. Making and grading the bar exam can't be fun. The only way to stand the process is to make it as easy as possible.

Thus, the examiners test the same issues over and over because it's easy. They don't want to get adventurous with the test and make it hard on themselves. The biggest curveball they'll throw you is testing a subject that hasn't been tested recently.

Flip through the old exams and see if you don't notice the same concepts popping up over and over. You can get a very strong grasp on the essays just by studying the past exams - and remember, a solid grasp is all you need.

Again, study the subjects that come up the most often. Play the stats to your advantage and focus your time where the money is. If Contracts shows up on one of the 6 Multistate Essay Exams 90% of the time, I'd make damn sure to memorize all of the legal issues tested on Contracts in the past exams.

If after looking through your state's past essay exams, you don't see the same issues tested with a strong frequency, bolster your essay practice by going over outlines of the most frequently tested subjects. The outlines will serve as an excellent backup to the knowledge you gain from repetitiously testing yourself. This will require more time, but states vary in how they test the law, with a few that try to work in law not regularly tested.

The great thing about essay exams is you can rack up partial points, and partial points can get the job done. If an exam question is worth a max of 25 points, 15 points is probably enough to pass you on that question.

To get a nice points base on the essays, all you need to do is answer the question, identify and define the directly applicable law, and include the facts in your analysis of how the law applies.

General Essay Answer Format

- Conclusion
- Legal Issues in Essay
- Define or Explain Legal Issues
- How the Law Applies to Fact Pattern
- Affirm Conclusion

For your exact essay format, study the approach taken in your state's essay model answers.

You're not trying to hit a home run on every essay. Getting on base with a single or even a walk works just fine.

Even if you know you're missing some key legal issues, give the best answer you can by following the format skeleton and filling it in with as much material information as you can.

Don't waste your time on long "BS" types of answers. Instead, directly answer what you have been asked with as much applicable law as you know – even if you don't know the exact legal terms.

My distinct impression is bar graders hate:

- BS answers
- Unorganized answers

- Answers with facts without analysis
- Answers that don't clearly answer the question
- Answers that don't include a conclusion

With this in mind, write essays that are 1) organized, 2) clearly identify and define the legal issues, 3) weave legal analysis and the facts given, 4) make a conclusion.

To find out the structure best suited to your state, take five model answers and identify the common scheme or pattern in how they were answered (e.g., conclusion issue rule analysis conclusion or CIRAC).

Another helpful hint is to look at the fact pattern and question closely and see what they're getting at or what direction (as far as legal concepts) they're trying to push you. Sometimes you can conjure a halfway acceptable answer by reverse engineering the fact pattern and question.

Also, it's very important that you DO NOT leave any essays blank. Essays are worth way too many points to leave blank.

Depending on how your bar is weighted, leaving an essay blank might be the same as leaving 17 MBE questions blank.

There's a decent chance I would have passed my second exam had I not left two essays virtually empty. I neglected these essays, trying to hit home runs on the essays I knew better, and then ran out of time before I could attempt a salvageable answer.

This leads to a very important point on essay exams:

Ration your time.

The Texas Bar Exam has 12 essays spread over 2 3-hour segments. Divided out, each essay theoretically should receive 30 minutes of time. This is not an accident. The bar examiners write every question so that each should take roughly 30 minutes to answer.

This means if you finish a "30 minute essay" in 10 minutes, you almost certainly haven't fully answered the question. On the other end, if it looks like you're on pace for 45 minutes, you're getting off on a tangent or including unnecessary law or analysis. Therefore, you should strive to keep your essays at or near 30 minutes each.

To find out how much time to ration for each of your essays, visit your bar exam information page and divide the number of essays into the time allotted.

I highly recommend you answer your essays in the order they come and try to have each wrapped up within 30 minutes (35 minutes at the latest).

If you're struggling with an essay, answer what you can as competently and quickly as you can and come back to it if you have time. You may remember more law as you run through other essays.

Note: I have only taken the Texas Bar Exam. Your bar exam essays will probably be different in some form or fashion. Tailor your study habits to the bar exam you're taking.

Remember: The safe blueprint can be found in the past essay exams and model answers. The best way to predict what will be on your exam is to study what was on the past exams. If you feel compelled to outline a few subject areas based on what you see, go for it.

Summary

Before the bar, I thought the essays would be the most daunting part of the exam but they're actually very simple questions that are extremely easy to answer. If you learn the laws most commonly tested on your bar exam essays and understand how to apply those laws to the desired essay format of your state, you're golden.

You will pass your bar exam by practicing the past 10 years' worth of essay questions. You will not only learn the necessary law, but you will see exactly how to format your answers the way the examiners want you to.

CH 4: THE MPT

The Multistate Performance Test (MPT) is non-substantive! Let me repeat that: The MPT is non-substantive! This means you don't have to know any law. All you have to do is write some sort of response (memo, letter, etc.) to someone (typically another attorney or a client).

Not one time did I ever write out an MPT response in studying for the bar. Never! Not only is the MPT non-substantive, but it's only 10% of the grade in Texas.

One key to the MPT is knowing how to write and format your response. For example, are you sending a memo to an attorney or a letter to a client? If it's to the client, you must convey the message in easy to understand terms, etc.

The other notable point on the MPT is you must be able to write your response in a clear and organized manner.

My advice for the MPT is to study the different formats and when to use them. This won't take you long. If you aren't comfortable with the MPT or want a better feel for it, just write out a few practice responses from past exams and check your answer against the model answers.

Some "experts" will say you should spend half your time organizing an answer (i.e., outlining) before you write it out. I never did. On the exam, I marked things I thought were important, took mental notes of other material I would need later, and started writing.

The MPT isn't difficult but you do have to keep a brisk pace throughout – well, at least I did. While swiftly moving through the folder of documents you're given, remember your objective: to identify and answer what you have been asked to identify and answer.

There will be additional information in the packet that you do not need. It is imperative that you leave unimportant information by the wayside. The MPT is largely an exercise that tests your ability to extract pertinent information from an array of documents and relay that information to the person you are addressing in a clear and concise manner.

If the MPT portion of your exam is worth 20%, it's worth your time to write out a practice response under timed conditions just so you can get a feel for how it works.

Otherwise, the bulk of your time studying for the MPT should be spent memorizing how to respond in different formats to different persons. Pay particular attention to header format, who you are writing to, the information you include or don't include (e.g., don't cite case law to clients), the voice you use, and the conclusions or opinions you include.

As for study time, I recommend you spend 4 hours total looking over the MPT. If you answer an MPT question, tack on another 1.5 hours. Once every 2 or 3 weeks, review an MPT guide and a few MPT questions just to ensure you're comfortable with it.

When studying for the bar, it never made sense to me how many people would pour hours into studying for the MPT. Don't invest in the MPT heavily because your ROI is capped.

Depending on the state, the bar exam usually comes down to at least 80% MBE and essay - and those portions are substantive, meaning you can't pass them without knowing material law.

DO NOT make the mistake of treating the MPT with anywhere close to the dedication you give to the substantive portion of the exam.

Summary

The MPT needs to be viewed and respected for what it is: a portion of the bar exam that adds points to your score. For this reason alone, it commands your attention. However, do not dedicate yourself to practicing this section of the bar exam. Rather, you should understand it.

To understand the MPT, review sample answers and memorize the different types of responses.

CH 5: PROCEDURE & EVIDENCE

Most states don't have Procedure and Evidence – or P&E – but Texas does. If your state doesn't, skip right over this section as it means nothing to you.

If you're in Texas, here's the quick breakdown:

Like the essays, P&E has major overlap from year to year. I studied P&E by reading the questions and model answers for about 6 years back. Many of these EXACT same questions resurfaced on the exam, but I will warn you that some questions I never saw also found their way to the test.

If you're in Texas, this whole section is only a 10% cut of your exam so I don't recommend going back and studying all of Texas Criminal and Civil P&E. I'd stick to the exams but go further back – 8 to 10 years – to try and hit on some of the more obscure questions they test.

I recommend studying for the P&E 1 to 2 times a week for 1 hour each session.

Tip: Absolutely do not write outside the answer lines you are provided.

Note: Laptop is not allowed on the P&E.

If you come across a question you have no clue on, guess to the best of your ability and move on. Remember, missing a few of these questions isn't a death kneel. This entire section is worth 10% and there are 40 total questions.

Summary

P&E is a straightforward section of the test. You will see many of the exact same questions on your P&E as were on previous tests. Thus, there is completely free money to be had simply by taking the previous P&E portions of the exam and then studying the model answers.

Study several past P&E portions and remember the bar examiners do like to mix it up on the P&E. If you come across an unfamiliar question, guess and move on.

CH 6: BAR EXAM TIPS

This chapter is a collection of tips that will help you during the lead-up to the bar exam.

#1 **Keep the bar exam in perspective**. Yes, it's a big test, but it doesn't make you or break you. It's not life or death (some people really do act like it is though). And the overwhelming odds are that if you study consistently for the previous 8 to 10 weeks before the test, you will pass.

If you don't pass, guess what happens? You live on and you take the exam again and you'll pass it then.

Don't burden yourself with panic, fear, pressure, etc. It won't help you for one second. Think about it: when is the last time worrying ever helped you with anything?

#2 **Study consistently**. A consistent study diet is so much easier than trying to shove 12 hours of studying in a day. If you use my techniques for studying and consistently average 4-5 hours a day on weekdays and 2-3 hours a day on weekends, you're in a great place.

You can start studying 8 weeks before the exam under this plan but if you want more security, start 10 (or maybe even 12) weeks prior.

Of course, you can take days off whenever you need to. Just make sure you study steadily throughout the weeks leading up to the bar.

Note: Cramming is highly inefficient because you need to expend more hours to learn the same amount of information. Your brain can only process so much information at a time.

You'll need less study time if you just study consistently in the months leading up to the exam. Studying 2-5 hours a day for 8-10 weeks is much easier than 10-12 hours a day over 2-4 weeks.

#3 **Exercise and eat well**. Even if this isn't something you do now, add some exercise and improved nutrition to your daily regimen. Your mood will improve. You will think clearer. You'll have more energy. And you'll feel better overall. This stuff really does help with the bar exam.

You don't need to set the world on fire either. Just walk for 20 minutes 5 times a week and/or try adding vegetables and brain foods (blueberries, salmon, avocados, mixed nuts) to 1 meal a day. It makes a huge difference.

#4 **Entertain yourself**. If you're putting in the study hours, you also need to put in the non-study hours. Watch movies, hang out with friends, play video games, play sports, go shopping, etc. Whatever it is you have fun doing (and don't have to think about), indulge yourself.

The cool thing about the bar exam is that because you're studying consistently, you also need to balance that with fun stuff. Ironically, it's the responsible thing to do. What you're doing is resetting your brain so you can study optimally.

#5 **Take breaks when studying**. After 50 minutes of straight studying, give yourself a 10 to 15-minute break so you can refocus. Don't stretch breaks to the point where you're out 30 minutes plus. Remember, it's just a break, not a stopping point.

#6 **Consolidate your time**. If you're studying, study. If you're having fun, have fun. Don't try to watch tv while you do MBE questions. Don't try to form a study group and then start talking to each other about non-bar stuff.

I'm actually against study groups altogether. I work much better at my own pace and without other people's input. I think most other people do too – even if the group is only talking about bar-related material. If you really need some help, you can always ask somebody for help without forming a study group.

#7 **Sleep well**. I didn't follow my own advice on this one (I stayed up to cram more info) but it makes things so much easier when you're rested and refreshed – both for studying and exam taking.

Your brain functions 1000% better when you sleep, so sleep! If you're well rested, you'll process information faster, you'll recall exceptions better, etc. Sleep alone can make the difference between passing and failing.

#8 Study during the lunch break. When we were let out for lunch at the half way point of our essay and MBE days, I studied in my car after listening to a few songs and eating some brain food. I mainly went over major topic areas that I had already highlighted as stuff to go back over.

To me this is free money that can't hurt you. Some people say you should rest up and relax. After giving myself 15 minutes of non-thinking, I can't just go mill around and chat while I've got a chance to review right before the second half of the test.

I heard someone say either you know it or you don't. My theory is I know it pretty well, but I can know it a little better by the time halftime is over. It can only help to look over some mnemonic devices or exceptions to the law right before round 2. This is especially true on essay day.

#9 Prepare everything the night before the exam. Clothes, pens, pencils, laptop, power cord, driver's license, admission ticket, lunch, breakfast, keys, gas in your car, etc. The last thing you want to do is forget something.

If you run down the checklist the night before, you virtually eliminate that possibility. We all forget things from time to time and if you're running late or nervous for the bar exam, it increases the chances you forget an item. Take those chances out by preparing your necessities ahead of time.

#10 Get to your testing center early. You don't want to play Saved by the Bell on the day of the exam. I was at the testing center at least 20 minutes early all 3 days.

This gave me one less thing to think about. Traffic became a non-issue. Parking became a non-issue. I could study in the car with the free time. There's no downside to being early.

#11 **Be comfortable in your clothes**. This is a you thing. I kept as comfortable as possible during the bar exam. I wore wind pants and a t-shirt with a sweat shirt or sweat jacket every day.

I saw one girl that went straight in her pajamas. It's all about how you feel most comfortable taking the exam. If this means slacks and a dress shirt, so be it. I recommend bringing something warm and easily detachable so you can adjust your clothing to fit the room temperature.

#12 **In between exam days, study for at least a few hours**. The Texas Bar Exam lasts for 3 days. After I came home the first and second day, I took a nap, ate, and then started studying the next day's material. I threw in running to give myself a study break.

The point here is the same as it was on the lunch breaks in the car. Why am I not going to look in the books while I have a chance? This is free time you have to prepare for the next day and look at the answers. Use it.

Some bar exam experts say you shouldn't pick up a book. I say you can pick up free points the night before. Plus if you get 8-9 hours of sleep, you'll be completely rested from the studying.

#13 **Set a million alarm clocks**. I don't know the feeling but I'd hate to experience waking up at 8:20

when the bar exam starts at 8:00. The night before the exam I set my phone alarm, my watch alarm, and my alarm clock. I also had 3 people texting me and calling me to make sure I woke up. Anything can happen so set your fail-safes.

#14 **Bring ear plugs**. I made a mistake here. People can either be totally oblivious or just not care about those around them.

The first time I took the exam, the volunteer proctors talked amongst themselves during the exam! I don't know if they thought they were being quiet but I could easily hear them 20 feet away. They just sat there chatting and laughing it up. After a few minutes of trying to ignore it and hoping they would stop, I finally got up and told them to stop talking. Nobody wants to be that guy but there was this little quiz thing going on.

The second time I took the bar exam, the girl next to me (as in maybe two feet away) whispered the MBE questions to herself. She was quiet enough so nobody else could hear but I could! It was extremely annoying but the only viable option at that point was to tell her before the second session started so I waited until then.

My third time taking the bar exam, a guy in the section ahead of mine (about 25 feet away) was bouncing his shoe on the floor and it was making a sticky/squeaky noise every time he went up and down. Before the second session started, the guy seated next to me told me he asked him to stop so that was taken care of.

The point here is I went 3 for 3 in distractions during the bar exam. I never once remembered to bring ear plugs but I highly recommend them for you. They can be a real difference maker in limiting distractions.

#15 **Don't talk to other people about the bar exam**.
Of course the bar exam is a hot topic but talking to
others about it doesn't really help you. If you listen to
your fellow bar takers, they'll saddle you with how
confident or unconfident they are, their paranoia, or their
unimportant thoughts on how to study.

None of it helps you. Many first-time bar takers love to
talk because they've got a lot of nervous energy, they
don't want to study, and/or they want assurances. They
either want to feel better about themselves by showing
how smart they are (possibly compared to you) or they
want you to reassure them and give them a pep talk.

Stay away from all of it. When you talk to other people,
talk about anything else but the bar.

If you have a question about the bar exam format or
local rules, contact your board of law examiners. If you
need advice, email me at kris@thebariseasy.com.

#16 **Don't bring your cell phone to the testing
center**. The closest your cell phone should get is in your
car in the parking lot. Some of you are addicted to your
cell phone. Don't bring it to the exam center, even if it's
on silent.

#17 **I recommend using your laptop**. Some people
like to handwrite. If this is how you feel more
comfortable, go for it. I recommend writing your exam
on laptop. Here's why:

First, you can potentially type much faster than you can
write. Second, your hands won't get tired or cramped

from typing. Third, there's no possibility you lose points for handwriting the grader can't read. Fourth, it's easier to erase and rewrite. Fifth, it's easier to organize your answers or make chronological notations.

The downside to computers is that blue screens and missing files can happen. This is rare and I would guess that less than 1% of laptop exam takers have a real problem, but the possibility is there. You can whittle this percentage down to next to nothing by using a problem-free laptop on the exam.

This means if your current laptop has problems such as shutting down unexpectedly, not saving documents, or other glitches, don't use it. I would either buy a new laptop specifically for the exam or borrow a friend or family members' working laptop for the next couple of days. Just make sure it's working with no problems.

#18 Consolidate your daily study material (e.g., essays or MBE) into 45-minute blocks. You might have the desire to switch what you're studying for whatever reason. I did. If you do, just promise yourself 3/4 hour of studying one subject or format before you switch. What this does is prevent unnecessary shifting around and forces you to at least accomplish at least 45 minutes of work before moving on.

Let's say you're tired of working through MBE and essays just sound more interesting. Try to make it through 45 minutes of MBE before you make the switch. You'll ensure you get in some MBE practice while also stopping any unnecessary delay tactics your subconscious mind creates.

#19 Mnemonics are extremely helpful on the bar

exam. Use mnemonics whenever possible during your study. Mnemonics are kind of like having a "lifeline" on the bar exam because they at least steer you in the right direction or give you a hint.

For example, my mnemonic for the elements of a negotiable instrument was SUFOON. SUFOON stood for:

1. **S**igned in writing
2. **U**nconditional
3. For a **F**ixed amount
4. Payable to **O**rder
5. Payable **O**n demand
6. **N**o undertaking

This mnemonic didn't cover every last detail but it gave me an easy structure I could recall to remember the elements of a negotiable instrument. Once I got rolling with the foundation, it was very easy to fill in the minor details.

This is why mnemonic devices are so helpful – they give you hints when you draw a blank.

Drawing a blank might happen. It happened to me on the bar exam. There were a few times where I simply couldn't remember the elements or definitions that I knew the essays were asking for. As soon as I was able to remember the mnemonic or just a few pieces of it, I was home free.

#20 **Worry about you and nobody else**. The bar exam is a you thing. You shouldn't worry about what other people are doing or not doing. It's almost always irrelevant to you.

Some people will study for 10 hours a day for 3 months straight on their way to the insane asylum. Other people will read celebrity gossip during their study time. Some people will look cool, calm, and collected while privately having a mental break down. Other people will look completely frazzled but have it all together. In the end, none of it matters.

All that matters is you and how you're doing. To this end, you can't pass the bar for anyone else and nobody can pass the bar for you. If you're waiting for a magical bailout from one of your friends, it's not coming. If you're trying to study for one of your friends, you're pulling yourself down. When you prepare for the bar exam, your job is to make sure you pass. That's it.

#21 **Bring a silent digital watch**. Believe it or not, my watch played a vital role during the exam. I actually attribute points to my watch because it kept me on pace each day of the exam. Without a watch, you only get the standard 15-minute and 1-minute-until-stop warnings (at least in Texas). With a watch, you know exactly where you are at all times. For example, if after an hour you're only through 30 questions on the MBE, you're 3.33 questions behind the pace you need to finish 100 questions in exactly 3 hours.

This information is extremely valuable in helping you speed up and correct pace. If you find out you're 10 questions behind pace 15 minutes until stop time, it's too late to correct course; You're going to have to rush through your last questions just to finish.

The reason I recommend a digital watch is because it's easier to see the numbers and calculate where you're at than an analog. If I glance at my watch and see 1:15:00

from the stopwatch setting, I know I should be approximately through 2.5 essays. In contrast, if I look at my watch and see 9:37, the time elapsed won't be as clear - especially if the exam started on a time like 8:19.

Note: Make sure the watch can be turned completely silent and is on silent when you take the exam.

#22 **Train proper brain endurance**. For most people, the bar exam will require you to be able to think critically for 3 straight hours. If you engage in focused, concentrated study (e.g., no Internet, talking, etc., during study) consistently during your study sessions, you will be able to go for 3 hours with no problems. Sprinkle in a few half or whole day simulated exam sessions (SES) and you'll be ready.

A half day of a SES would be taking a practice exam for 3 hours straight. A whole day would be 1 3-hour practice exam with a 1-hour break and then another 3-hour practice exam.

#23 **Don't freak yourself out**. Some bar takers get way too worked up about the bar exam. They end up crying in the bathroom, skipping the second day of the bar exam, or as part of some other folklore.

First of all, there's no sense in getting this emotional about the bar exam. If you allow yourself to get this worked up, it's self-sabotage and your worst fears of not passing might come to fruition. If you're worrying yourself to failure, what good does it do? Just stay calm and try your best. If your emotions are running high in the weeks prior to the exam, drown your anxiety in MBE and essay questions.

#24 **Find a balance of # of study hours**. There is such a thing as studying too much for the bar exam. If you find yourself at 12+ hours per day, I think you're studying too much.

The law of diminishing returns applies to your study time so you must be able to think beyond "study = good". I've created this graphic to illustrate my point:

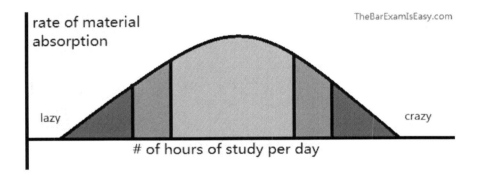

As you can see, at some point your reward for time spent studying starts to decline. This has nothing to do with being irresponsible and everything to do with being human: Our brains get tired of thinking after a while.

As your study time goes further and further to the right, your material absorption rate deteriorates and becomes inefficient to the point where you're actually wasting your time by continuing to study.

As I've mentioned, it's critical to factor in the quality of your study time. The more focused and concentrated your study time is, the less hours you'll need to study. The more fragmented and diluted your time is, the more time you'll need to study.

What the Bar Exam is Like

I've taken the bar exam in two locations in Texas. I've also heard accounts from friends in other states. From my experience and what I've heard, the bar exam is mostly what you would expect.

You arrive at some sort of convention center or warehouse-like setting and check in at the entrance. You will then go to your assigned seat. You will probably sit at a table with someone else. The tables will be arranged in some fashion with laptop takers in one section and hand-writers in another.

Every morning the proctor will begin reading the instructions. After the instructions are read and everyone is ready, the exam will begin and you will forget about everything else.

In Texas, nobody can get up until 15 minutes has elapsed after the start time. After 15 minutes, you can get up and go to the bathroom or get a drink.

Once time elapses on the exam session, you stop work and wait for everyone to shut down their computer or have their exam collected. Once the proctor is satisfied that everyone has been accounted for, you will be released. In Texas, if you finish 15 minutes or more prior to the end of the session, you are allowed to leave early.

During lunch breaks, many people talk to each other. Some will go somewhere to eat while others will eat and/or study in their car.

CH 7: THOUGHTS

To close the book, I'd like to informally discuss some theories and thoughts I have towards the bar exam.

Leverage The Past

The reason I say the bar exam is easy is because the answers are right in front of you. By and large, all you have to do is practice the previous exams enough times to where it'd be hard not to pass.

20 samples of your test (2 for the last 10 years) are readily available to you (not the Multistate). You can learn the subjects that are always on the exam, the subjects that largely tend to be on the exam, the subjects that are sometimes on the exam, and the subjects that are rarely on the exam. From there, you can decipher the probability of what concepts will be on the exam and will not be on the exam.

The power in this information is that you are already privy to what will most likely be on the exam. With the bar exam graded on a pass/fail basis, you only need to be proficient on most of the exam. Knowing this, it's very conceivable that you could simply play the percentages and allocate almost all your time to the money concepts and get the job done.

Concentrated Study Time

The bar exam is only about the concentrated time you put in, not the total time you put in. There are bar takers that will "study" for 400+ hours and fail while other bar takers put in 90 hours or less and pass.

The difference usually has much less to do with intellectual capability and much more to do with effective use of study time.

Worrying about the bar exam isn't studying. Browsing the Internet with your book in front of you isn't studying. Talking to your friends about the bar exam isn't studying. Going to get something to eat isn't studying. None of this counts. It's all fluff. Just because your book is in front of you doesn't mean you're studying.

Studying means actually studying. Not feigning to study or doing something in between studying.

If you take this to heart and string together 2-5 pure and concentrated study hours per day, you will very likely pass if you start studying 8-10 weeks prior to the exam.

Drop Distractions

Ignore your red herrings and concentrate on simplicity. You may have heard of red herrings on the MBE but have you thought about the red herrings you create on your own?

There will be any number of things that come into your field of vision during the bar exam. Unless someone's health or freedom is in serious jeopardy, whatever is going on is not that important. Don't create distractions and don't seek them out.

Don't worry about the latest flashy study materials from the bar exam courses. You don't need them.

Don't worry about your DVR not catching your favorite show. You can watch it later.

The list goes on but my point is to free your mind of distractions and to concentrate your focus on this straightforward and simple test.

Less Anxiety

If you have anxiety, try your best to release it. I wasn't nervous about the bar exam but I understand you may be. If you are, I've got the cure for you: Practice more MBE or essays.

The best way to get rid of your fear or nervousness is to build confidence. You can build confidence by logging concentrated study time consistently within the week.

The earliest you should begin studying for the bar exam is 3 months out. If you start this early, this will help release any extra pressure you may have because you'll have peace of mind knowing you're preparing far in advance.

Because you're an early bird, you should max out your

study time at 4 hours per day for the first month. After the first month, you can take your average up to 5 or maybe even 6 hours per weekday should you desire an ultra-thick security blanket.

Bloated Prep Courses

Bar courses have to bloat their courses to justify their price. You know how you legitimize turning the same video lectures and copies of books into $3,000 year after year? You add bells and whistles. You cover every last shred of law in the state. You puff your chest out and exclaim for all in the land, "OUR COURSE IS THE BEST".

Unfortunately, all the apps, flash cards, attorney essay graders, video lectures, question banks, and whatever else are conveniences at best and distractors at worst. I have told you exactly what you need to pass the bar exam. You don't need anything else.

Another unfortunate aspect of bar review courses is they cover unimportant material. I must have heard "but you don't need to worry about that for the bar exam" (or something to that effect) at least 20 times during the video lectures. Several times this will be uttered after 2 or 3 minutes of rambling on about the unimportant information. ARE YOU INSANE!?!?

If something isn't important or it's never on the bar exam, don't you dare waste my time telling me about it during a bar review course.

But bar exam courses do, and the reason why is they know how law students can be. Someone will inevitably fail the bar exam, construe how some remote piece of law could have possibly saved their score and complain about it to the world. This is why bar courses cover just about everything possible even when they know many areas of the law will never be on the test.

This is another reason why bar courses are inefficient means of preparing for the bar exam: They prepare a review to satisfy every last person rather than what is practical in terms of passing.

Last, the surety of success is continued discipline. Most of us will not do something until we absolutely have to. In studying for the bar exam, it is vital that you are able to sit down by yourself for at least a few hours 5 to 7 days per week and study. You must be able to keep this pace for at least 2 months.

This study is not a torrid pace. It is an easy, tried and true pace. The bar exam rewards steady, consistent studying over a few months' time, not hurried, rushed studying in the last few weeks.

This is not to say a fast and furious push in the last 3 weeks cannot succeed. It can. However, waiting until the last month of preparation to kick your studying into "serious" mode is a mistake. You will not experience the same comfort level as more disciplined studiers and your margin for error will diminish.

Many bar takers will enroll in a bar prep course simply for the structure and it may indeed provide you the framework you need. However, you will need to exercise discipline in your study habits regardless of whether or not you take a bar review course. Read: You will have to study by yourself. Enrolling in a bar review course and attending isn't going to pass you by itself.

Bar review courses don't pass the bar. You do.

Digging Deeper

I had an email exchange with a bar taker that made me realize I hadn't fully explained my methodology in this book. Moreover, I thought other parts of this Q & A could be helpful to readers. As such, I've added most of the contents (with edits) from those emails here.

Note: The questions from these emails are in italics with my responses underneath each one.

I just finished your book. "The Bar Is Easy." It's helped to relieve some stress, but I'm a bit confused as to how to go fwd. My exam is July 29th & 30. I'm enrolled in [bar course] and started going to the lectures on Tues. It seems you advocate not attending lectures and doing loads of questions. So I have a few questions:

1. Since I've already spent +$3K and cringe at the thought of spending any more, can I use the materials given instead of buying the last 10yrs of [state] Bar questions? I'm thinking that they prob have encompassed all the past questions in their materials.

I haven't used the [bar course] MBE questions. I have gone through the Kaplan MBE questions and I thought they were representative of the bar exam questions. Also, for The Bar is Easy, I researched alternative workbooks and found the reviews compelling enough to recommend the additional practice questions listed on MBEPracticeQuestions.com.

Because of this, I recommend Kaplan and other highly rated MBE questions. However, I don't want to sway you against [bar course] (especially since you already paid for their materials) and have you go out and unnecessarily buy more MBE questions. I do urge you to make sure other recent bar takers are happy with the caliber of MBE questions.

2. It's day three and I am already "behind" even in your study plan. Should I try to do three sets of 36 MBE Qs or just start from here?

This is completely up to you. The reason I say it's up to you is because I don't want to box you into my mentality. Obviously, I like my pace but [bar course] has their own recommendations that have worked for a lot of people. If I were you, I wouldn't try to play catch up all in one day. I'd add 10 MBE questions every day and try to get on track with at least [bar course's] pace.

3. I don't know the substantive law yet. Should I: a) study the outlines a bit first; b) get as much as I can from the classes and then just start doing questions; c) just start doing questions and create an outline from the answers; or d) some weird variation of any of the above?

When I tried to learn substantive law from the lectures and outlining, it didn't carry over well onto the practice questions. Yes, I knew more of the substantive law but I didn't know how to apply it to what the questions were asking.

What worked best for me was learning the pertinent law and how it was tested directly from the questions and not even worrying about studying the outlines. If I had to take the bar exam in July, I'd do this again.

This is not for everybody (maybe you learn better outlining beforehand) but I think studying directly from the MBE questions saves time and is more effective for learning the law.

4. Also, how do I balance [bar course]'s suggested schedule with your own?

I don't know [bar course]'s study schedule but if I were taking the bar exam, I'd follow my study schedule. My study schedule gets right to the point because you're not outlining or watching lectures.

The hardest part about long days where you begin by watching lectures is it takes away from your ability to focus. After a few hours of lectures or outlining, it's natural that your attention starts to wane. That's why I think it's better to focus on what reaps the most rewards.

Thanks for taking the time to respond to my questions. I think this information would help in making the book more complete. What frustrated me was the "how;" such as how exactly do you go backwards and learn the pertinent law from just doing the questions. I know you said to make an outline from the questions, but it seems it would be pretty disjunctive. Another fear is how do you know that you are not missing pertinent information by just learning from the questions and not the complete outlines.

As for how I learn the law by answering the questions, it's the repetitious reading-answering-checking them that drilled the pertinent law into my head.

Learning the applicable law was a natural result of the consistent repetition. As I did more questions, my scores progressed.

What I found was that after I did so many questions, the tested material law repeated itself. While the questions were usually framed differently or made you undergo a deeper analysis, the underlying substantive law stayed the same.

Con Law was the one area of law where even after 100 questions, there was something new that would come from nowhere.

Other than that, most of the tested material completely flatlined after 100 questions. And even before that, you'd see the same law tested again and again.

This is an incomplete hack in that there might be a question that comes up that you haven't come across the law before. But the reason I go the straight question route is because:

1. You learn the vast majority of the issues the bar examiners like to test
2. You learn the way the substantive law is tested
3. You allocate your time to #1 and #2 rather than outlining the black and white law

The MBE is tricky, not because of the law tested, but because of the way it's tested. At the beginning of my bar study, there were many times while answering the question that I knew the law being tested but I still didn't know the answer.

The reason is the MBE on the bar exam is typically

either layered or deceptive. Thus, I think the best way to study is to learn how MBE questions are designed/structured through repeated practice. While doing this, the material law part comes fairly easy.

As for the fear of missing out on some of the material law, I knew I was never going to learn all the law. Fortunately, learning most of it well and how to apply it on the questions is all the bar exam requires. I could see from my practice exam scores that my scores were well above what was average or necessary to pass.

When you know you're taking bar exam level difficulty questions and scoring high enough to pass, it gives you the confidence/knowledge that you're on the right track and don't need to worry about missing out on a few questions here and there.

Addendum

After dozens of emails and phone calls with bar takers, particularly those within the last year, I've added this section to The Bar is Easy in hopes of quelling anxiety and putting the bar exam in better perspective.

Hero vs. Loser

What throws off bar-takers isn't the extensive material or the study time - it's the binary outcome: You're either a hero or a loser; there is no in between.

Those who pass revel in celebration with family and friends.

Those who fail get pity pats on the shoulder and consolatory hugs while they figure out how to trudge through awkward exchanges with passers and askers ("How'd you do on the bar exam?").

This is partly why passing can be so euphoric. And this is partly why failing can be so disappointing.

But when you get away from all the human emotion and simple-mindedness, you're not a hero if you pass (unless you get some insane score) and you're not a failure if you fail (unless you have no business being an attorney* and/or didn't study).

*If you graduated from an accredited law school, odds are you very much have business being an attorney.

Anxiety

The binary nature of the bar exam amps up anxiety for all bar takers and then amplifies disappointment for those who fail.

Imagine if leading up to the exam I told you that if you pass you get $100,000, but if you fail you get $0. That's going to ratchet up your anxiety, even if you study your heart out. And that anxiety may change how effective your studying is.

However, if I told you that the bar exam is scaled on a basis of $0-$100,000 and you'll be awarded with an amount proportional to how well you do, you'll still have anxiety, but it won't have nearly the same edge because you will still be compensated to some degree proportional to the work you put in.

When it comes to academics, we don't like all or nothing, and we certainly don't like the accompanying uncertainty that goes into an all or nothing result.

Process

Knowing that the bar exam ends with a binary outcome, and you can't achieve that outcome with 100% certainty, the most you can do is to incorporate the best process possible.

The reason I wrote The Bar Exam is Easy is because I believe(d) the prevailing process (how to study/practice) was extremely flawed and was thus decreasing the chances of passing.

With this addendum, what I'm advocating is that you channel your efforts and energy into creating the best customized process and forgetting about the result (pass/fail) as much as possible.

What many of you are looking for is the perfect boxed process – there is none.

Neither the bar courses nor I can offer you the perfect study plan tailored to your predilections. You must assemble the best process based on 1) your knowledge of how you optimally learn, and 2) researching and incorporating bits and pieces of process strategy.

The reason I believe the core philosophy of my book is worthy is because it's aligned directly with the source: I don't deviate away from the exam itself in advocating what to study/practice.

What I recommend is that you invest several hours into

researching and customizing the best process for you and then as you study and practice, fine-tune your process to better optimize material absorption and thus give you a better chance at a passing score.

Look at everything you do leading up to the bar exam as a chance to improve your percentage chance of passing but understand that just because you've done everything to give yourself, say, an 80% chance of passing, it doesn't mean you will, in fact, pass.

Luck

There are chance elements involved in the bar exam and, yes, luck is a part of the equation. You can reduce the role luck plays with increased study time but it's still there.

Examples of luck:

Example 1: Pretend passing is 675. You get a 668. I get a 675. We both blindly guessed on 8 MBE questions. I got 4 of my guesses right. You only got 1.

Example 2: We both study in our car during the lunch break. I study an essay that appears word for word on the second essay in the afternoon session. Nothing you study helps you.

This section is merely to acknowledge the potential of luck to radically alter the outcome of the exam.

This is not to say you're lucky if you pass or unlucky if you fail. It just means sometimes luck is involved, especially on an exam where everything can turn on a single point.

Failure

People fail the bar exam at a fairly high rate. If you belong in this category – like I did – work on improving your process so that you can increase your percentage chance of passing on your next attempt.

If your score is significantly lower than your passing cut off, you need to carefully scrutinize why you are so far off. If you waited too long to start studying, then there's an obvious fix for that. However, if you can't pinpoint why your scores are so low, solicit objective opinions on why you're so off.

Most law schools have counselors available who can help with this.

Shame

There is so much self-inflicted shame for those who fail the bar exam. People seriously act as though they have done something embarrassing by failing the bar exam.

I want to reiterate that you should not feel ashamed if you made a good faith attempt to pass the bar exam and failed.

Also, it's worth reiterating that the nexus between your ability to pass the bar exam and your ability to competently practice law is extremely weak.

To get away from shame, you have to get away from emotion and from simple thinking.

I know, if you pass and get to run in the door and hug mom and dad while your siblings realize what happened and join in, and everybody jumps around and celebrates, I'm a jaded idiot and this paper metaphorically gets crumpled in your hand and tossed to the wayside.

But, if you fail, take solace in the logic I've laid out and take measures to play the percentages on your next attempt.

The guy who scored 16 points higher than you and passed isn't a regional hero despite all his Facebook friends and family glory.

And despite missing the cut off by 10 points, you aren't a complete loser who needs to run away and escape all the incoming pity-shame.

There's no hero and there's no loser. It's just two people who took the bar exam. One did a little better and passed. The other needs to improve their process and pass next time.

To get even more analytical, here's a raw attempt at making passing the bar an equation.

You + Process = Pass or Fail

The "You" and Process components are what drives the results, but both are subject to extreme variables.

You = intellect, memory, attention span, work ethic, distractions, time available, anxiety level, pre-knowledge.

Process = number of questions practiced, types of questions practiced, consistency, concentrated time, environment.

The more variables within each component that are favorable to you, the more likely you are to score higher than the minimum competency score and pass the bar exam.

At this point, most of the "You" variables are fixed but you may be able to improve factors like distractions.

The Process is completely up to you so you can maximize your output here and drastically improve your chances of passing.

Should you fail the bar exam, re-evaluate your process so you can make changes, improve, and have a really high chance of passing on your next attempt.

A Virtual Lock

If you want to make sure you pass the bar exam, the checklist below will virtually guarantee you a passing score.

First, practice 2,800 MBE questions.

Second, practice the last 10 years of essay questions three times.

Third, study consistently.

Fourth, don't worry about the test.

That's it.

Note: This is for those that want complete assurances. By no means do you need to study this much to pass.

One Opinion

Take this book for what it's worth to you and remember where the words are coming from – one person. My information contains bias just like anybody else's information does.

Also, I did not ace the exam. I passed the exam. This means that I have experience in passing the exam (one exam) but I am not an expert in every last testing area.

What I'm getting at is this book isn't necessarily an end all, be all. This book is my best attempt to convey to you the most efficient (save time and money) and effective (pass the bar) way to pass the bar in my opinion. You should use the information in this book so as to best help yourself. My advice isn't meant to corner you into a regimen or a mindset; it's merely to share what I believe is best.

For most states, my recommended study time amounts to approximately 280 hours over 10 weeks. This averages out to just 4 hours per day - and even 4 hours a day is probably more study time than you need.

Bar review courses indirectly suggest much more time through their recommended study. I would too if I inundated you with an array of fluffy apps, flash cards, flow charts, outlines, video lectures, audiobooks, and other indirect study methods. However, I don't need to justify charging you thousands of dollars, so I have told you exactly what you need to pass the bar exam and nothing more.

If you think anything I have written is garbage, by all means throw it away. If you think something in this book is money, take it all the way to the bank.

Your bar exam study must be 100% about what helps you. If you find any study material or method to be ineffective, toss it.

Final Thoughts

If I haven't deflated the bar exam hot air balloon for you yet, how about we just face your biggest fear, that you fail the bar exam.

You know what happens after you fail the bar exam?

You sign up for the next one and pass it.

Everything is really simple and straightforward if you just stop and look at what they test. All you have to do is study the right information consistently and you're going to pass.

So there you have it, the monster is dead. The hype is gone. There's nothing to fear anymore.

The bar exam is easy.

BAR EXAM BEACH

ELIMINATE STRESS FROM THE BAR EXAM

Kris Rivenburgh

Bar Exam Beach

Bar Exam Beach was a separate guide to alleviating stress and anxiety concerning the bar exam.

I've now included this guide in The Bar Exam is Easy.

ABOUT

Bar Exam Beach was written specifically for bar takers that desire a stress-free bar exam experience.

In this book, I thoroughly dissect the simple elements of the bar exam so you can see how unintimidating the bar really is. In addition, I provide a best practices guide for passing the bar exam. I also provide a practical outlook for those with time constraints (full-time job, kids, etc.).

Bar Exam Beach Explains:

- Why bar takers fail the bar exam
- The approach that will pass you
- What to do if you go "blank" on an essay
- Why a bar exam blueprint is huge
- How to never feel like you're missing something
- Why you shouldn't talk about the bar exam
- How to catch up if you've fallen behind
- What healthy foods can help you study
- How to relax throughout your bar experience

The objective of this book is to eliminate all mystery and ambiguity concerning the bar exam so that you can be 100% confident in your preparation. With the right preparation, you need only put in quality, consistent study hours to arrive at Bar Exam Beach.

Once you reach the beach, there's nothing to fear and no reason to worry. You can shed any anxiety or stress as you dip into your MBE practice book with the water touching your toes.

HOW TO VIEW THE BAR EXAM

The bar exam is an extremely straightforward test (with the exception of Michigan's 2012 July exam). All you need to do is condition yourself for it and you will pass.

Look at the bar exam as a test of your ability to learn and recite the key areas of law in your state's preferred format.

For example, if your state uses the Multistate Essay Exam (MEE), and Criminal Law is a frequently tested subject, all you need to do is 1) learn the law by practicing past essay questions and 2) learn the proper response format your state prefers from the model answers.

You will see that the Criminal Law material breakdown and proper format is very mechanical and completely straightforward (same as any other subject). You will also discover that the same major issues continue to pop up.

While practicing questions, you will build foundational knowledge to every testing section and the underlining subjects, issues, and sub issues.

The graphic below illustrates how structured and straightforward the essay portion of the bar exam is.

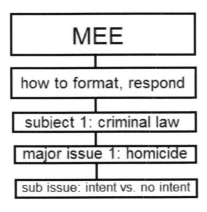

This is all the essay portion of the bar exam is and ever will be: a breakdown of major issues and sub issues within the different subjects.

The MBE portion is even easier. Just practice bar exam level difficulty MBE questions and you will be 100% ready for the bar exam MBE.

The MPT or PT is merely an exercise in understanding what is asked, extracting the pertinent information from relevant case law or statutes given, and responding to the task given with a clear and organized answer in the proper format.

When you take the exam, about 60% of the essay law you studied will be on the test. The MBE will be a test of your MBE practice question work ethic. The MPT or PT will grade your analysis, comprehension, and organization skills.

If you study the right way, consistently for the prior 8-10

weeks, you're going to pass.

Depending on what state you're in, you may have one more section worth a small fraction of your grade, maybe 10%.

That's all there is.

Squares and Circles

I created circles and squares as a way to think about your approach to preparation.

Circles are anything that takes away from your studying.

Squares are everything that contributes to your studying.

Remove all of the fluffy, emotional, unimportant, and unnecessary circles from your bar exam experience. They have no place in studying for or taking the bar exam. Rather, studying for the bar exam should consist of foundational, linear, direct squares.

Do you remember that diagram from 20 seconds ago? That's your just like bar exam preparation: simple, mechanical, and straightforward.

9:30 am MBE questions

11:00 am Essay practice

12:30 am Lunch

1:00 MBE questions

2:00 Rest of your day

This is your new, temporary schedule for the next 2-3 months.

It's simple. It's straightforward. It's easy.

Bar takers that fail cloud their life with circles. They

infringe upon the structured bar exam lifestyle with an emotional and/or fluffy lifestyle.

Lifestyle circles include: personal dramatics, relationship problems, gossiping, partying, and competing interests.

Studying circles include: extended breaks, multi-tasking, watching TV, Internet browsing, day dreaming, going out to eat, and talking.

Bar takers that pass adopt a squared, structured regimen. They have definitive objectives and let nothing stop them.

Lifestyle squares include: exercising, eating right, planning ahead, prioritizing study time, and making necessary adjustments.

Studying squares include: scheduling consistent bar study time, tracking MBE improvement, reading the official bar website instructions, limiting breaks to 10 minutes, studying alone, and selecting an appropriate study environment.

Your chances of passing the bar exam skyrocket when you take a bottom-line, punch-clock approach to studying. Plan how you will study (subject, time, duration, place, eat, etc.) and then execute that study plan with no excuses. If something forces you to alter your plans, account for that change and get back on schedule.

When you're not preparing for the bar exam, indulge yourself in whatever you want so long as the activity doesn't negatively affect your study time.

Hangovers negatively affect you.

Example: You drink so much on Saturday that you're sick all of Sunday and don't feel like studying.

Relationship problems negatively affect you.

Example: You decide to tell your girlfriend all her flaws. You argue and then spend the next week worrying about a potential break up.

Adding competing interests in your life negatively affects you.

Example: You decide to compete in a triathlon two weeks after the bar exam so you begin training for it. You now have 12 less hours in your weekly schedule, taking away any spare time you had. You also have something new tugging at your attention.

The point: Stay away from distractions and don't create any.

The bar exam is a simple, structured, dry exam that rewards consistent preparation. There is nothing emotional about the exam so don't add any emotion to the process.

FIXED DETRACTORS

You have kids. You have a full-time job. You have kids and a full-time job. You have kids, a full-time job and a medical condition.

None of this changes anything. You still develop a plan to prepare for the bar exam and execute it.

You may have more going on than most bar takers, but these are fixed conditions in your life and you must account for them in your schedule.

You're not after sympathy (sympathy doesn't pass the bar exam). Your only objective is to adjust your bar pass formula to account for the fixed conditions that already exist in your life.

You may have to divide your studying into four one-hour-long segments. You may have to add additional study time on the weekends. You may have to sacrifice recreational activities.

What is certain is that you have to develop a study plan that allows for an adequate amount of quality study hours.

The more detractors you have that take away from your bar preparation, the more difficult it is to prepare for the bar exam. This is simply a fact you have to adjust to.

Think of it this way. Some people have poor eye sight while others do not. Those with poor vision get contacts or glasses so they can have good vision. They adjust because of a fixed condition in their life.

Bar takers with fixed conditions must do the same.

Building a Strong Foundation

Two days before your formal start date for studying, read your state's bar exam website instructions thoroughly and map out exactly what you need to do.

Make notations of important information like:

- what sections are on the test
- how the sections are weighted
- how much time is allotted per section
- what sections/subjects are tested
- the proper response format

You need to have a crystal clear idea of exactly how to study before you start studying. Leave nothing to ambiguity. If you have any questions, call or email the state bar. If you have any questions on the best study approach, solicit opinions from recently licensed attorneys.

If you leave nothing to the imagination, you know exactly how to plan for the bar exam and pass it.

Example 1: If you know your MPT or PT is only worth 10%, you can adjust how much study time you allot to it. Clearly, you will not want to give it anywhere near the attention you do essays or MBE.

Example 2: If you know how much time you have, on average, to answer each question, you can tailor your study habits to quicken your practice pace or even slow down if you're rushing.

Planning ahead of time with a strong foundation alleviates any uncertainty you may have and allows for you to be fully confident that your preparation is directly on point to pass the bar exam.

Many bar takers fail the bar exam every year, not because they don't study but because their preparation isn't directly aligned with passing the bar exam.

You will save hours of time in your bar exam preparation by studying correctly.

Chapter 5: Beautiful Seclusion

In the weight loss arena, people are looking for a silver bullet; that magic pill or exercise routine.

Many bar takers are after that same silver bullet. Perhaps a bar review course, a magic outline, or a study group will carry the day?

The solution to both is continued effort towards your goal.

To pass the bar exam, study the right material, consistently, by yourself.

Nobody can pass the bar exam for you.

Acknowledge this fact right now.

Consistent, concentrated study passes the bar exam

every time. Not bar review courses. Not study groups. Not legendary outlines. Consistent, concentrated study.

Consistent, concentrated study is sitting by yourself and practicing the bar exam every day, for 2-5 hours per day with no Internet, no TV, no talking, no going out to eat, no phone calls, no texting, and no multitasking. Just straight studying with 100% focus on practicing the bar exam.

Note: You need to study when you're awake and highly functional.

Tip: I highly recommend you study in a well-lit room by yourself.

Think of your study time as your excuse for complete seclusion and isolation, a chance to get away from all the noise in the world and just focus on your personal enlightenment.

When you leave your seclusion for the day, divorce yourself completely from it. Your study time belongs to that study room and nothing else.

I recommend you attempt to 100% forget about the bar exam outside of that study room. Put the bar exam in its place. The bar exam is not your life. The bar exam is something you study for for a few hours a day.

For this reason, don't discuss the bar exam with your friends or family. Remember, you don't need to because you already know exactly what you need to do (the foundation you built prior to studying).

Friends from law school will want to talk about the bar

exam with you.

"What did you get for #57?"

"Do you think the McNaughton Test will be on there?"

"I seriously think I'm going to fail this test."

"I'm getting 80% on my MBE practice tests every time."

"I'm spending two hours a day on the MPT."

And on and on.

Do not put yourself through this. None of this matters to you.

Talking about the bar exam wastes valuable non-study time – or even worse, actual study time.

Talking about the bar exam might make you second guess yourself (e.g., I'm only scoring 55% on my MBE; I'm way behind).

Talking about the bar exam might take you off course (e.g., maybe I should study for the MPT more).

Do not allow this.

You developed a rock solid blueprint for passing the bar exam. Follow it.

You will give enough hours of your life studying for the bar exam. Do not give any more idly talking about it.

Health

For your brain to function at optimal levels, you need nutrition, exercise, and sleep.

Strive for 8-9 hours of quality sleep if possible (the bar exam is a great excuse to buy that awesome pillow you always wanted).

Exercise for 20-40 minutes 5 days a week. Walking works. A combination of strength training and cardiovascular exercise is wonderful. Just try to get your blood flowing and build a nice sweat. Doesn't need to be anything spectacular.

Feed your brain with some quality food. Water and roasted raw almonds or walnuts are a great study partner. Also try to incorporate blueberries, spinach, wild salmon, avocados and other high-quality foods into your diet.

If you have the big 3 (nutrition, exercise, and sleep) working to your favor, studying will become much easier. You will absorb and retain information at a higher clip.

Health is a real difference maker in passing the bar exam.

Correcting Course with Less Than a Month to Go

Some of you may be up against the clock as you read this book. You either started studying late or you've studied for weeks and still feel completely unprepared. Both of these predicaments are completely normal.

There's no sense in looking back, all you can do is do your best going forward.

Don't worry, your chances of passing are still very much alive.

The best course of action is to assess where you're currently at with MBE and essay subjects and create a study blueprint to try to bring your weakest subjects to at least average scores while maintaining your strengths.

For example, if you're strong on Torts (60% correct rate) but weak on Contracts (40% correct rate), practice 15 Contracts questions and 7 Torts questions per day.

Note: Remember, this is a strategy for those with limited study time.

I highly recommend abandoning any outlines or lectures (these aren't effective means of studying, anyway) and concentrating your study time solely on practice questions.

You can definitely pass the bar exam with a late start. You will need to ramp up the study hours but with a strong finish, I like your chances of passing.

Test Days

When you actually take the bar exam, you have every reason to be confident that you will pass the bar exam. You took care of the preparation end and now it's time to reap the rewards.

Before each test day, make sure you have everything set up for a seamless experience. Create a checklist so everything goes your way.

Here is a sample checklist:

- Car is fueled and working
- Clothes are prepared (including flex clothes to adjust to temperature)
- Laptop is working (if taking laptop exam)
- Laptop power cord is packed
- Earplugs are packed
- Pens and pencils are packed
- Food is prepared or taken care of
- Water is accounted for
- You have your bar ticket
- You have your driver's license
- Your alarm clock is set
- Your fail safes (e.g., wake up phone call) are in place
- You know exactly how to get to your testing center
- Study materials for your break (cheat sheets, etc.) are packed

Plan to arrive to your testing center 25-30 minutes early to make sure not even horrible traffic can stop you from being on time. You don't want any artificial stress creeping into your perfect blueprint right as you're about to reach the summit.

The actual testing center is very mundane and unintimidating. You will be assigned a seat in a room of bar takers. Before the bar exam is administered, they will read you instructions and guidelines (e.g., bathroom breaks). Once instructions are read, they will hand out the exam. It will look very familiar to what you have studied for the past two months. You will then dominate the bar exam.

If you draw a blank on an essay question, know that this happens to many bar takers. If you have no clue whatsoever, skip to the next question and come back to it. If you have any semblance of an answer – no matter how sketchy – provide the best skeleton of your essay format (i.e., CIRAC) and fill it in with as much as you can and move on. If you have time, come back and try to write in a more complete answer.

On MBE questions, absolutely do not get bogged down on any one question. If you get stuck, I recommend filling in your best answer choice and leaving a check mark next to the number so you can come back if you have time left over. Remember that all 200 questions on the MBE are worth exactly the same. It's not worth sacrificing time on the easier questions to go all out on a more difficult and/or longer question.

During your breakfast and breaks, make sure you get ample water and nutrition so that you can perform optimally during the exam.

Practical Advice

Too Tired

If you're tired, take a nap. There's no sense in forcing yourself to study through problems when you're not learning anything anyway.

Sometimes all it takes is 15 minutes and you can regain focus and get back on track. It's better to let yourself recharge for 15 minutes to an hour than drag through problems when you're not mentally awake.

Kids

For those of you that have kids here's what I recommend:

When your kids are most energetic, exercise with them. This way you get the exercise you need while at the same time wearing them out. They're probably not going to come home and fall asleep but at least now you've expended some of their exuberant energy.

After that, give them food, drink, and a movie so they're occupied while you study.

Obviously it's not the best of study environments but you do what you can. Try to have a few days a week where you study without having to keep an eye on the kids. On these days, really max out your study time.

Challenging Exercise

Exercise will benefit you the most when you challenge yourself. If you're going through the motions with a slow walk, it's great you're exercising but you'll get more reward by pushing yourself harder.

Preparation = Confidence

If you have great study sessions for 2-3 hours a day, you deserve to be really confident about the bar exam.

The opposite is true if you've got 10 hours of junk studying a day. You don't need to put in this much time. It's almost impossible to string together 10 hours of great study time in a day anyway.

Prepare by putting up big numbers of practice questions. You'll learn the law and know exactly what the exam sections will be like.

Summary

When I was taking the bar exam, I was surprised by how many good students were rattled by the bar exam.

I knew they were going to pass because they were putting in the study hours. Yet, I believed in them more than they believed in themselves. You could tell they were legitimately not sure whether they could do it.

I think it all goes back to the monster under the bed thing. Your mind grows the bar exam into this huge, scary thing when it really isn't.

Why do we believe in the monster? Because we're told there's a monster over and over.

There is no monster. Yes, it's an expansive test and, yes, it requires dozens of hours of practicing the test - but it's really not that bad.

Think of how saturated the legal market is. Do you really think there would be so many attorneys if the test was as scary as everyone makes it out to be?

Stress can result from many things but in the case of the bar exam, it comes mostly from uncertainty.

This is why I urge you to turn over all the stones before you start studying. This is why I encourage you to practice questions like the ones on the actual exam.

If you know exactly what's coming and prepare for it accordingly, how much stress can you really have?

Come up with your study game plan. Set aside time to

practice. Follow it up with actual practice. Take the test. Pass it. Done.

I know you're not looking forward to the next 2-3 months of study days. I wasn't either, but in retrospect, it was just like a part-time summer internship; a couple months of 2-4-hour study days. That's all bar exam prep is.

I took days off when I felt like it. I still had time to workout and go out with friends. I slept great. I got some cool new stuff (laptop, pillow, watch, DVDs) all in the name of helping me with the bar exam. Really wasn't bad at all - nothing like I had made it out to be.

The Beach

I know this guide hasn't sounded very beach-like yet, but after 20 minutes, you've finally arrived.

Now you can imagine yourself on a white sand beach with gentle, clear blue waves touching your feet as you practice your MBE questions.

Stress, anxiety, worry…why? All you have to do is follow your blueprint and you will pass the bar exam.

If you're ahead of schedule or on schedule, you are in great shape.

If you're running behind, there's still plenty of time to catch up. Stay extra disciplined going forward and you will succeed.

There's nothing to worry about anymore. You know exactly what you need to do and how you're going to do it.

BAR EXAM EXTRAS

MBEPracticeQuestions.com links to MBE workbooks with good reviews. It's my site and I write all of the posts.

Everything else including a video companion guide to this book, updates, and social links can be found at TheBarIsEasy.com.

You can contact me at kris@thebariseasy.com.

ABOUT THE AUTHOR

I try not to let algorithms predict me too much. And my reps always end in even numbers.

You can read more at KrisRivenburgh.com.

Made in United States
Orlando, FL
20 September 2023

37100625R00059